Contents

Chickens live here

Most chickens live on farms. These chickens roam about outside. They are called free range. They are fed grain but also scratch the ground to find seeds, insects, **grubs** and worms.

What is a chicken?

Chickens live together in a group called a flock. The male is called a cock.

comb

beak

wattles

long tail feathers

claws for scratching

The female is called a hen. The cock chooses a hen and dances around her with one wing held out. After they **mate**, the hen will lay some eggs.

Laying eggs

The hen finds a clean, dry, quiet place to make a nest. When she is about to lay an egg, she clucks, fluffs up her feathers and squats over the nest.

The hen lays one egg each day.
She keeps laying until she has
a **clutch** of seven
to ten eggs.

Keeping the eggs warm

The hen sits on the eggs to keep them warm. She turns them around several times a day to keep them warm all over.

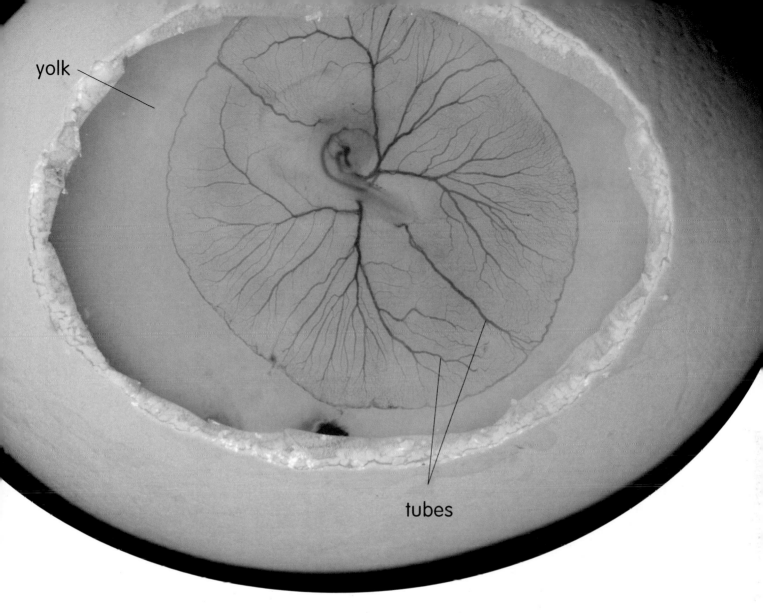

yolk

tubes

A chick begins to grow inside each egg.
The egg **yolk** is its food. Air comes
through holes in the egg shell. The red
tubes carry air and food to the chick.

Hatching

Every day, the chick grows bigger.
After three weeks, it fills the egg.
It has a sharp bump called an
egg tooth on its **beak**.

It taps the egg shell
with its egg tooth
and makes a hole.

It keeps tapping.
The hole
gets bigger.

The egg shell cracks and breaks apart and the chick **hatches**.

It is wet and tired from pushing so hard, so it rests in the egg.

1
hour

Chicks

The chick stands up and shakes itself dry.
Its body is covered with soft, fluffy **down**.

The hen waits for all the eggs to **hatch**. Then she leads the chicks out of the nest to find food. If a chick loses sight of her, it cheeps loudly.

Learning

The chicks go everywhere with their mother. She shows them how to drink and what is good to eat.

1 day

At night, they hide under her wings to keep warm and safe.

Growing up

The chicks grow bigger and feathers grow on their wings. They still follow their mother about. She shows them where to **roost** and how to avoid danger.

10 weeks

The chicks grow feathers all over.
They find their own food now, take **dust baths** and run around by themselves.

12 weeks

Cockerels and pullets

By now, chickens have a **comb** and **wattles**. Young males are called cockerels.

14 weeks

A young female chicken is called a pullet.

5
months

Adult chickens

Now the chickens are fully grown.
They are able to produce young
of their own.

Chicken life cycle

Eggs
The hen lays a **clutch** of eggs in a nest.

Hatching
The eggs **hatch**.

Adult chickens
Chicks have become grown-up hens and cocks.

Chicks
The chicks learn how to find food.

Glossary

beak the hard part of a bird's mouth

clutch a group of eggs that a hen lays

comb the fleshy red crown on top of a chicken's head

down the light, soft feathers of chicks

dust bath a chicken's way of cleaning its feathers by flapping around in earth

grub the soft, young stage of some insects

hatch to come out of an egg

mate when a male and female join together to produce young

roost to sleep at night

wattles the two red flaps that hang under a chicken's chin

yolk the yellow food sac for a growing chick inside an egg

Index

The life cycle of a
Chicken

Ruth Thomson

WAYLAND

First published in 2007 by Wayland
an imprint of Hachette Children's Books
This paperback edition published in 2009 by Wayland

British Library Cataloguing in Publication Data
Thomson, Ruth
   The life cycle of a chicken. - (Learning about life cycles)
   I. Chickens - Life cycles - Juvenile literature
   I Title
   571.8'18625

Editor: Victoria Brooker
Designer: Simon Morse
Senior Design Manager: Rosamund Saunders

Printed and bound in China

Wayland
A division of Hachette Children's Books
338 Euston Road, London NW1 3BH

Photographs: Cover main image, 6, 7, 16, 22, 23
Aflo/naturepl.com; 2 Ulrike Schanz/naturepl.com;
4–5 Thomas Fricke/Corbis; 8, 23 Bartussek/ARCO/
naturepl.com; 9, 10, 12, 13, 14, 17, 18, 23 Jane
Burton/naturepl.com; cover right centre, 15 Corbis;
cover top right, 11, 19, 23 Wegner/ARCO/naturepl.com;
20, cover bottom right, 21 Bengt Lundberg/naturepl.com

ISBN: 978 0 7502 5874 6

Wayland is a division of Hachette Children's Books,
an Hachette UK company.
www.hachettelivre.co.uk